Y++

Y++

I0024854

ISBN 9781736362037 © 2024 Nick Peterson - Old Nick and published by
DiaryUnlimited an Imprint of The Edge Press.

Contents

Y++ The Negative Dimension 5

The Precise "Y" (why) of life. 7

Exhibit 1 11

Exhibit 2 12

Exhibit 3 13

Exhibit 4 13

Exhibit 5 14

Exhibit 6 14

Exhibit 7 15

Exhibit 8 16

Exhibit 9 16

Exhibit 10 17

Exhibit 11 18

Exhibit 12 18

Exhibit 13 19

Exhibit 14 20

Exhibit 15 20

Exhibit 16 21

Exhibit 17 22

Exhibit 18 23

Exhibit 19 24

Exhibit 20 24

Exhibit 21 25

Exhibit 22 26

Exhibit 23 26

Exhibit 24 27

Exhibit 25 27

Exhibit 26 28

Exhibit 27 28

Exhibit 28 29

Exhibit 29 30

Exhibit 30 30

Exhibit 31 31

Exhibit 32 31

Exhibit 33 32

Exhibit 34 33

Exhibit 35 33

Exhibit 36 34

Exhibit 37 34

Exhibit 38 35

Exhibit 39 36

Exhibit 40 37

Exhibit 41 37

Exhibit 42 38

Exhibit 43 39

Exhibit 44 39

Exhibit 45 39

Exhibit 46 40

Exhibit 47 40

Exhibit 48 41

Y++ The Negative Dimension

1995.

AI

The Negative dimension is a three-dimensional space: a geometric setting in which three values: parameters are required to determine the position of an element (i.e., point). This is the informal meaning of the term dimension. The world consists of two dimensions: The Positive and the Negative. The Negative dimension is like an unprocessed side of what used to be a photographic picture.

The Positive is the world in full colour where we are supposed to live. In reality we're not. We live in the Negative. We never die there.

Thousands of years of living creatures are all living in the Negative dimension. It's never ending whereas in the Positive dimension, we only have one life.

After a car crash in London, in 1995. X1 went into a coma and when he woke up, he began to experience a series of hallucinations referencing the letter Y.

X1

Among entries that caught my attention as indubitable clues per se, but baffled me in respect to their order of appearance were the questions revolving around the vicinity of personal infringement of my dream. I recollect this quite clearly. Were you dreaming/ Did it hurt/ furthermore with insufferable insistence: did it hurt a lot/ How badly did it hurt/Have you suffered much/Who did you meet/Where were you/were you dreaming in colour? And amongst the chaos of this inquisition, I heard them garbling and muttering between themselves: "It is very rare to dream in colour, black and white is more common. We shouldn't have had exceeded the dose! "What does"? I'm still questioning myself on the subject.

AI

The Precise "Y" (why) of life.

Y++. Far beyond the Solar System: impossible situations. A series of sketches about the miseries of life in the 21st century and its effects on the human condition. During the course of the action, the negativity is gradually replaced by positivity, turning misery into a mere passing necessity thus providing a guide to surviving the unexpected.

X1

That's how it happened. It's all true for everything that has been lived through and currently happening as I'm typing these lines. But when you read these lines, I'll be long dead, unlike X2, who's alive, young and everything else that comes with it. If you have the time, you can go back and back and back and start counting the Ys used in this story...' 'This is how it happened. Y++ is this organic map of the universe. Y1 is the positive dimension; Y0 is the negative dimension in binary terms equal to that of the Y+ and Y- in the positive electromagnetic jargon. I don't feel like anything or anything feels like me anymore. I'm invisible, this ubiquitous character that never ceases to grow. I'm here, there and everywhere at the same time, where everywhere is somewhere and somewhere is nearer than that from the nearest entity. An omnipresent sentiment that flows and reflows in constant motion at the speed of Y. Y speed is faster than the speed of light, as it isn't speeding at all. "It" doesn't have to. It is here, there and everywhere. It is the shape of the universe, where the infinite is suddenly finite and measurable in terms of Y. There is awareness of where it begins and where it ends. Y is the only entity that defines itself: everyone has got that symbol engraved somewhere in the far cell of their brain, and growing. This is evolution.

Evolution sucks, though. It happens just because it did. I remember watching endless documentaries on the origins of the universe. The earth was revisited by overpowering volcanoes making way to tons of water, then a few islands, then some plants, then fish, animals, humans, then this, then that and then all this and that gathered together at the speed of a snail gliding slowly along on the grass. All this goes beyond the point of tolerance and acceptance. It all goes on and on and on. In fact, in real terms, it doesn't. We live what we live, we suffer what we suffer, bear and wear what we could as long as we can because we do; it's just something that we do. We always play to the best of our own abilities. We've never tried to do otherwise or dare to think differently. Thinking could be digressing and digressing is another form of pain and pain is a disturbance, a sub-pain. I wouldn't know how to think the right way or how to go about it but I just know that things just are and become and happen. What I know is that evolution is truly *finitesimal*, not infinitesimal. It seems long but it isn't. The images seen on the endless documentaries about the origins of life on earth are somewhat distorted. Things indeed did happen.

Whilst a fish struggles to grow some legs at the speed of a snail gliding slowly over the grass and begins to walk, some other worlds, in another dimension at the same place, same position in time, things happened: other things of a completely different speed, faster than the speed of light, at the speed of Y.

At a glance, the images aren't speeding at all. They seem stagnant and still and yet, they are speeding. So, when I think about this silly documentary about human's evolution that moves all right, but since it took so long to get there, the whole episode brings back to me that snail slipping slowly over the grass. The whole saga only tends to convince me that there is, somehow, somewhere, something fundamentally wrong. Perhaps it is that this slow-motion of being is not very cost-effective, that there is always something skulking behind another, and that the old physic principle, one of my traditional adages: "to every move corresponds a reaction from an equal and opposite force". I've never tried to be neither too scientific nor too vague about that subject, but this is more than just assumption, but real detective work, a certain logic based on existing knowledge and this inherent intuition that is omnipresent in cases like these. No religions involved, purely self-scent, not belief. But still much more than just guessing, as guessing assumes the unknown, "it" doesn't feel it or smell "it" or have "it".

This map of The Universe has one definition: Y and even more Y++. It is no longer a god, because it is an entity and it is no longer infinite as it can be defined and measured. The dint of this obsession is finally out. The veil has been lifted on this accident, such a mysterious accident. So mysterious that the deepness of his absence (coma) prompted disagreeable surgeons to perform some viewing of his left brain and left puzzled some *neuropracticians* and other *mnemotechnicians* on the series or words and numbers scribbled down on the back of 25 different hospital meal menus.

In all, it was some stories about some people, somewhere in time, guided by my arrival. I became both the conductor and the trigger of these virtual animations and everything else came to fit and move on accordingly. One has to learn that one doesn't age anymore as the spirit is the same forever and never and merely the physical aspect changes. Until it vanishes away and in perfect simultaneous coordination, another self-creature is resurrected with a different appearance. The spirit remains the same and the interaction goes on and on forever and never until somehow, somewhere someone in time precisely at the same geographical and geometrical location will decide otherwise. And when one is convinced about this liberty of achieving so, one will undoubtedly become part of this different place somewhere in the negative dimension. One might be able to get back to the board game of the positive dimension, and play and play back and back and again and again and again, again, again, again, again, again, again, again...'

AI

Far beyond the Solar System: impossible situations...when the negativity is gradually replaced by positivity, turning misery into a mere passing necessity thus providing a guide to surviving the unexpected.

Exhibit 1

Y-X1: The Y-chromosome

Y-X2: You have not paid your bill. You have now been taken to court and lost and taken to a debt collector. You are now required to pay your bill immediately, failing that the bailiffs and sheriffs will come over to your home to collect your belongings.

Y-X1: A dead man's body is spluttered with blood, one cold morning: a nobody who slept in the park the previous night, in London like so many.

Exhibit 2

Y-X1: Y-chemical symbol of Yttrium

Y-X2: You are hit by a new tax bill: the demand is obviously wrong as it is 10 times bigger than normal and you have not earned more money than the previous year. After the initial shock, your anger is brewing and you phone the tax office. After screaming at the waiting line for nearly an hour you hang up the phone saying that they were on strike and couldn't get through. You have lost a day of your life.

Y-X1: The universe is governed by the rules of the periodic table, there is one periodic symbol in particular above all the others that can change the course of history.

Exhibit 3

Y-X1: Y -in algebra it is the second unknown quantity.

Y-X2: Still chasing your tax demand, you decide to write a complaint by registered post. After hearing no news for 3 weeks and receiving a threat from the debt collector, you write another letter to the tax office and the debt collection agency. You have now wasted 3 weeks of your life.

Y-X1: A lesson in Algebra, a key element of the notion of time and time as reflected.

Exhibit 4

Y-X1: Y-in geometry, it is the second coordinate.

Y-X2: Following a miscalculation by the tax office, they are now taking you to court. After wasting another hour holding over the phone, someone is answering the phone. You are extremely stressed out and still coherent but the tax inspector on the line is adamant that you must pay. You raise your voice and the inspector is asking "are you being rude?" and hang up on you. In all, you have wasted 30 days of your life.

Y-X1: A lesson in geometry, a key element of the

notion of space and time as reflected.

Exhibit 5

Y-X1: Y-shaped thing, an arrangement of shapes in lines

Y-X2: After a miscalculation by the tax office and a huge demand, the bailiffs and sheriffs are now on your doorstep. You have called the police who managed to save you. The problem is referred to the court and you win. No excuses from the tax office or compensation and it will take them another six months to amend the bill after many reminders from them to pay and many more letters from you. You have wasted 6 months of your life!

Y-X1: The third and the fourth dimension.

Exhibit 6

Y-X1: Y-Yeomanry.

Y-X2: You are a citizen of a war-torn country and from one day to the next your country is run by different dictators from either left or right edge of the political spectrum. Your country is oil-rich so everyone is trying to loot the land depriving you and the natives of the means to survive, let alone live.

You are only 16 and you have always known this situation. You have already wasted 16 years of your life.

Y-X1: The act of submission and servility to the authority.

Exhibit 7

Y-X1: Y- abbreviation of YEAR (S). Y=year(s).

Y-X2: You are a citizen of a rich country but at war and there is no food.

The country is run by a dictator. The Western world is keen to help as it is oil rich so they decide to bomb the country. The bombs have just destroyed your home, your family and friends. You have nothing and nothing left to lose so you escape for a better life by walking to the far away country that bombed your country. Your journey will last 3 months and you have wasted another 3 months of your life.

Y-X1: How long does it take to become oneself?

Exhibit 8

Y-X1: Y- Mediaeval numeral: Y=150, Y=150, 000.

Y-X2: You are a refugee from a war-torn country and are desperately trying to enter a promised land. You are being kicked out many times by the border guards. You are forced to live in a refugee camp infected by rats and diseases and receive left overs for food. You survive one month until one day you manage to break into the country. You are then arrested and thrown into a prison then a refugee camp. You will stay there for two years and during that time you are applying for asylum. Eventually you are free to go and live in the country. You have wasted 18 years and three months of your life.

Y-X1: King Arthur.

Exhibit 9

Y-X1: Y-moth, any of the genus of destructive noctuid moths with a silvery Y-shaped mark on the forewings.

Y-X2: You have just been fired from your job. You haven't got any savings left and your wife needs money for the maintenance of your new baby. You are unable to find a new job and you apply for unemployment benefits. The situation at home is getting more complicated and your wife is suffering from postnatal depression. After 3 months, unable to cope, you turn to alcohol and start smoking heavily. Your wife kicked you out of your apartment. You ask for help from the welfare office but it has been denied. You are now sleeping rough in the streets. So far you have wasted 3 months of your life.

Y-X1: The Flight of the Moths.

Exhibit 10

Y-X1: Y (ggdrasil)- in Scandinavian mythology, an ash-tree whose roots and branches join heaven, earth and hell.

Y-X2: You are at the ATM and have just realised that there is a problem with your bank account and you are overdrawn for a huge amount. You immediately run home to call your bank. After waiting for 50 minutes over the phone, someone based in a faraway land answers the call but cannot speak good English.

Y-X1: Wizard 3: The tree of life.

Exhibit 11

Y-X1: Y-fronts.

Y-X2: After another twenty minutes you are being transferred again to another person who can't really speak English either but is very nice and is trying his best to help and eventually manages to solve the problem: your account has been hacked, someone managed to steal thousands from your account and another 30 minutes on the phone and you are told that you need to wait another 24 hours for everything to return to normal. You have wasted an hour and forty minutes of your life and adding to this you are blocked from using your bank account for 24 hours.

Y-X1: What makes a man a man.

Exhibit 12

Y-X1: Y-(HVH)- with added vowels: Jehovah, the Hebrew name of God in the Old Testament. So, named in Yahwistic (Yahvist), the postulated author or authors of parts of the Hexastich, which God is regularly called, by this name.

Y-X2: You had your bank account hacked but have managed to stop everything over the phone with your bank. The following morning when using the ATM, you realise that the problem has not been resolved. You run to the bank and start queuing to see a cashier. After twenty minutes of great distress and rage, you are told that you are overdrawn without permission and the bank may close your account if you do not repay the overdrawn balance immediately.

Y-X1: God?

Exhibit 13

Y-X1: Y- symbol for admittance.

Y-X2: You explain the situation and the cashier advises you to call customer service. By this point you explode and the security guards throw you out of the bank. You then try to call and wait another two hours over the phone and you are promised that everything will be back to normal within 24
hours. You have wasted the previous day, another day and the new promise of a resolution for another 24 hours, 3 days in total.

Y-X1: Being finally acknowledged and accounted for in data.

Exhibit 14

Y-X1: Y-bar. A crystal bar cut in 2-sections, with its long direction parallel to Y. A piezoelectric plate cut from a quartz crystal in such a way that the plane of the plate is perpendicular to the Y-axe of the crystal.

Y-X2: After 3 days of being told by your bank that the hack and the loss of thousands from your account will be sorted out, a letter from the bank
arrived stating that since you have overdrawn the account, the bank has been forced to close the bank and sent the account to a debt collecting agency. The agency will then add their compensation, court and agency fees on top.

Y-X1: A huge fire devastated an entire land and many forests. Hundreds of people and animals died. How did it start? Why did it start? How to comprehend the meaning of this?

Exhibit 15

Y-X1: Y- capacitor. A radio interference suppression capacitor intended
for applications where failure of the capacitor could lead to danger of electric
shock.

Y-X2: You are in agony: this is the end of the month; your bills and rent will not be paid and you are forced to borrow from your friends and family. On the advice of a friend, you rush to the regulator ahead of the court summons. After two weeks the regulator rules in your favour, orders the bank to pay you compensation and remove you from a black list, preventing you from opening a bank account elsewhere. In all you wasted 17 days fighting the bank and another week trying to open a new bank account with another bank. A total of 24 days has been stolen from your life.

Y-X1: The government has mismanaged the economy. It decides that the next best option is to invade another country and plunder its resources. Thousands will lose their lives and many more will seek refuge in the country
that made them homeless.

Exhibit 16

Y-X1: Y-circulator. A circulator consisting of 3 identical rectangular waveguides joined in a symmetrical Y-shaped configuration with a ferrite post or wedge at the centre. Power that enters any wave guide emerges from only one adjacent wave guide.

Y-X2: The hospitals in your country are using an agency to clean and this agency sub-contracts the job to some refugees with very low wages. The job of cleaning a hospital is an extremely technical and skilled job. As a result, many hospitals are left in filthy conditions with blood stains remaining on the walls of operating theatres for weeks on end.

Y-X2: There are billions of aliens and extraterrestrial forces circling around the earth and time-travelling at the speed of light around the various universes. What does it all mean? Do they know us?

Exhibit 17

Y-X1: Y- the total ease of altering current flow at a given frequency and voltage. The reciprocal of impedance. A quantity, which in rectangular form is as useful for parallel circuitry as independence, is for circuits. The resultant of conductance and subsidence in parallel. The resultant of reciprocal resistance and reciprocal reactance in parallel.

Y-X2: Many patients die as a result of contracting an infection. Your parents and children have died as a result. It has taken 5 years to get over the loss and start rebuilding your life. You may have wasted your whole life as a result of health regulations that allow a complete disastrous management.

Y-X1: Is the only role for a woman in life is to bear children and satisfy men or can a woman thrive and have an orgasm, especially after the menopause?

Exhibit 18

Y-X1: Y-admittance expressed in Siemens (S) or into (X-1) x is the omega sign and the - is on a bit higher.

Y-X2: Your new electricity bill is astronomical: more than your mortgage. You try to phone the energy company every day for a week but no one is answering the phone. You then discover an email after an hour of navigation through the company's website. You email the company. A week later and on the same day you receive: a red reminder, an email acknowledging receipt for the email and the bailiff turns up on your doorstep.

Y-X1: Britain has one of the highest pregnancies among girls in the age group 12-15 and this is even more prevalent in the ethnic population. The government seems unwilling or unable to tackle the problem.

Exhibit 19

Y-X1: Y=Y=Y magnitude.

Y-X2: In desperation you file a complaint with the regulator, it has been accepted and any action taken against you has been stopped. Three months later a new bill -even more astronomical- has arrived. On the same day, an email explaining that the electricity firm offers many plans arrived and I had not chosen one and I was on the most expensive one.

Y-X1: An average man has the highest sex drive among all primates and miles apart from its female counterpart. Can this drive be tamed and controlled? The Y wizard scrutinises the problem.

Exhibit 20

Y-X1: Y-defection. Vertical deflection of the spot on the screen of a cathode ray tube. (Xdeflection).) Y-diode. The decoding diode in each of the Y Ines of a memory matrix. (Xdiode). Y=phase angle of admittance before y is the O with a bar across "th" symbol.

Y-X2: They are now offering you a new affordable payment plan each month. You have wasted 3 months of your life arguing and fighting and have been swindled of thousands that you are still repaying every month for years to come.

Y-X1: Since the introduction of the bicycle for all, London has been invaded by all manners of bike schemes and 1 dead cyclist and one dead pedestrian a day or a week.

Exhibit 21

Y-X1: Y-polar.

Y-X2: You are hit by a cyclist who is speeding over the pavement rather than on the road. You are just managing to put yourself together when suddenly you fall over another cyclist and have just avoided being run over by a truck. The police and the ambulance arrive on the scene and one unfortunate cyclist is taken to hospital.

Y-X1: The population of the UK has been swamped by huge influxes of Eastern European peoples, already immersed with huge migrations from Africa and Asia. How is it affecting the British population?

Exhibit 22

Y-X1: Y-rect.

Y-X2: Three months later you hear back from the incident, the cyclist has recovered and is suing you for reckless walking. Completely dumbfounded and bewildered, you seek advice from a lawyer and arrive a month later at the courts.

Y-X1: Britain claims to be part of a global world where so many things seem to be run from overseas in countries like India and China with call centres where no one understands each other.

Exhibit 23

Y-X1: Y-a. admittance. -b. Young's modulus

Y-X2: The driver in the van would have been in the wrong as he was driving when his car lights were red and the cyclist would have been in the wrong for ignoring the traffic lights but they are both desperate for compensation.

Y-X1: Is homosexuality a disease that can be cured and can the subject be re-orientated towards a healthy lifestyle?

Exhibit 24

Y-X1: Y-defection. Vertical deflection of the spot on the screen of a cathode ray tube. (X deflection)

Y-X2: The police can't get hold of the nearby camera footage and the cyclist lost both legs. You may be in for a prison sentence as well. You are now starting to get heavily depressed even believing that you may have done something wrong start ordering some prescription drugs to alleviate your anxiety.

Y-X1: The police and ambulance sirens in the UK are the loudest and most piercing in the world causing mass afflictions of Tinnitus and schizophrenia among the population.

Exhibit 25

Y-X1: Y-diode. The decoding diode in each of the Y Ines of a memory matrix. (X diode).

Y-X2: Another month has elapsed and you learn that two unexpected witnesses from the nearby school have tried to contact you in vain as the police refused to give your details. The two witnesses have found your address by accident by reading the details in the local newspaper where your lawyer's name has been published.

Y-X1: Britain has one of the highest amounts of drug consumption -legal or illegal- in the world, a huge drink and smoking problem. Is anyone bothered?

Exhibit 26

Y-X1: Y-drive. The driving source of energy for the y lines of a computer memory matrix.

Y-X2: On the day of the trial, the two witnesses explain that the driver was running like a maniac when the lights were red and he was followed by the cyclist. The cyclist fell underneath the wheels when the truck driver reared back.

Y-X1: Are computers, tablets and phones saving or destroying humans' life?

Exhibit 27

Y-X1: Y-gain. The gain of the vertical channel of an oscilloscope or X-Y recorder.

Y-X2: You have now won your case and as soon as

the judge handed over the verdict, you weep profusely in the courtroom. You didn't win any compensation and a week later arrived the shared bill for the court case and your lawyer's bill. You have wasted 4 months of your life, thousands in legal fees and are now addicted to painkillers.

Y-X1: Smoking kills but is vaping a solution or is it more dangerous and another new form of pollution for everyone in the streets?

Exhibit 28

Y-X1: Y- intercept=the y coordinate of the point at which a time or plane intersects the y-axis.

Y-X2: You are a gay man. You now have every right: smoke in excess, drink in excess, party, take drugs and get married. So, you do it all. You find a partner and you get married. You can also have children so you decide to adopt. After months of pick and choose, trials and errors, the adoption agency is choosing the two children that you will adopt.

Y-X1: The majority of people in any given country have become overweight and obese. Who is to blame? Who is triggering the pandemic?

Exhibit 29

Y-X1: Y-matched independence antenna (WYE antenna).

Y-X2: You adopt two 5-year olds. Three months later, it turns out that your adoptive children were children of heroin addicts and have been infected with aids. They need constant care. Another three months later and your partner can't cope with the situation and files for divorce. Taken by surprise you are divorcing without understanding the consequences. You end up with two children needing constant care, need to work full time and you are now on 60 cigarettes a day.

Y-X1: The average human being is riddled with addictions. How can anyone control its addictions?

Exhibit 30

Y-X1: Y-sink. The circuit or device into which the Y-lines of a memory matrix feed. (XSINK).

Y-X2: Three months later and you are fired from your job for having missed too many days at work. Another three months later, riddled with debts you have been diagnosed with cancer. Unable to face it, you commit suicide by swallowing various drugs.

You die at the age of 35 and your two adoptive children end up back in care. You have lost 35 days of your life and broken the hope of two innocent children.

Y-X1: Religion: good or evil?

Exhibit 31

Y-X1: Y-injunction. A waveguide whose longitudinal axes from ay.

Y-X2: You are running a small business. Despite taking all the necessary steps to insure your business against nearly everything and in spite of the fact that your office is located inside one building with security guards at the door, someone has managed to enter, stole some laptops, cash and valuable documents.

Y-X1: Migration and immigration: understanding the weather since the dawn of mankind.

Exhibit 32

Y-X1: Y-shear. A subsidiary fault in a shear zone parallel to the shear direction.

Y-X2: You file a complaint to the management company of the building for compensation but you are being turned down. You then file a claim to your insurance company and are being turned down as they are stating that the responsibility is shared between you and the owner of the building.

Y-X1: I do not believe in a government.

Exhibit 33

Y-X1: Y-was a command on the Apple Macintosh computer -now obsolete- to remove a disk.

Y-X2: You end up buying new computers with your own money but refer the matter to the regulator who dismisses your complaint. Many months later, when your insurance policy is due for renewal, you are being refused the policy for being a "high risk". You then try another insurance company and are being turned down again for the same reasons as you have been black listed. You have wasted 6 months of your life, thousands to replace the equipment and will never be able to be insured ever again.

Y-X1: Why is it that the most useful and logical item or action even law in life is being discontinued?

Exhibit 34

Y-X1: Y- plate, one of the two deflections electrodes that deflect the
electron beam vertically in an electrostatic cathode-ray tube.

Y-X2: You are finally in an age to receive a new smartphone and you end up using it all the time. At the end of the first month the bill is so huge you need the help of your parents to pay, not understanding why on a fixed contract you could end up with such a huge bill. The next month the bill is twice as much as the previous month.

Y-X1: Electricity and energy consumption: has the earth finally run out of the basics?

Exhibit 35

Y-X1: Y-factor. A noise measurement factor for specifying the noise figure of a receiver. It is based on known cold and hot reference temperatures.

Y-X2: This time your parents won't help, having already enough problems with their own phone operators. You decide to go to the regulator but the waiting time for a response is one year. Your phone is then cut off and your operator refers you to a debt

collection agency then the court. You then
repay twice as much in court and agency fees. You are
still awaiting a complete itemisation of the calls.

Y-X1: Is the world run by an evil sect?

Exhibit 36

Y-X1: Y-match. Also called a delta match. A method
of connecting to an unbroken dipole. The
transmission line is faced out and connected to the
dipole at the point where the impedance is the same
as that of the line.

Y-X2: After paying over £4000 in total for two months
you end up with a new £10 a month, pay as you go
plan and start becoming more aware of how to use
your phone. The next month you are bombarded with
texts from your new operator to upgrade to a £20
package but you won't change.

Y-X1: Why is procreation so violent?

Exhibit 37

Y-X1: Y-punch on a Hollerith punched card, a punch
in the top row, two rows above the zero row.

Y-X2: You discover that you have bad blood pressure and you thought you were hearing noises and voices in your head. A friend of your parents diagnosed you with Tinnitus. You end up learning to live with a new condition. You wasted 3 months of your life, over £4000 and generated a new condition as a result.

Y-X1: Do we really need governments to run the world or exist?

Exhibit 38

Y-X1: Y-Signal. A luminance transmission primary which is 1.5 to 4.2 MHz wide and equivalent to a monochrome signal. For colour pictures, it contributes the finest details and brightness information.

Y-X2: You have just received a completely incomprehensible demand for your gas bill that you cannot possibly afford. You never had one like this in 5 years. After waiting for 66 minutes over the phone, after the countless menus and sub menus that are looping back to where you started, after hearing the same music played back in a loop you are getting seriously agitated.

Y-X1: Why are we alive? Are we really alive?

Exhibit 39

Y-X1: Y-Signal. B: a signal transmitted in colour television containing brightness information. The signal produces a black and white picture on a standard monochrome receiver. In a colour picture, it supplies fine details and brightness information. It is made up of 0.30 red, 0.59 green, and 0.11 blue.

Y-X2: You suddenly hear a voice saying: "What do you want?" confounded you reply: "Is this the gas company?" "Yes, what do you want?"
And you reply: "May I give you an account number?" and the voice replies "Yeah?" And you reply: "Ok, now, can you please tell me why the bill is so high?" And the voice responded: "Are you raising your voice at me? Are you
being rude?" and then you hang up the phone refusing to escalate the problem further.

Y-X1: Visual communication: what do we see? What do we really see?

Exhibit 40

Y-X1: Y-Symbol of Tyrosine.

Y-X2: A year later you are still awaiting to hear from anyone about the problem, your gas bill has tripled. You cannot cope with the constant increases in your monthly bills. You have taken on another evening job but are still unable to pay for your family. A friend advised you to come with him to a betting shop. You start betting on horses. You lose but this is only the first try so you try again. You have just received your salary. You bet again and win some money and you are so happy; you decide to bet again and you win more money.

Y-X1: Can an AI or Artificial Intelligence really exist or is it only a machine with one or many humans hiding behind?

Exhibit 41

Y-X1: Y-bus. A matrix which contains the admittance of each element in
an electric power-system.

Y-X2: You bet again but sadly this time you have lost everything. A week later you have been made redundant from your job. Unable to cope, you start drinking heavily. One night, you have been so drunk and after a disagreement with your wife and 5 years old son, you push them both over the window of your apartment and they both die.

Y-X1: Is a man or woman (human being) really a cannibal (meat eater) or can he or she be vegan?

Exhibit 42

Y-X1: Y-parameters. The input and output admittances that are used to characterise a two-port device (network).

Y-X2: A while later, after more alcohol, the sound of the police and ambulance can be heard in the streets. You decide to end your life and jump out of the window. You were 30 years old. You have lost 30 years of your life, killed your wife and child.

Y-X1: In the 21st century, do we really need a democracy and is there any point in voting?

Exhibit 43

Y-X1: Y-connection. A three-phase source or load, which is connected such that the elements are connected in parallel and are thus, represented in a schematic diagram in a Y or star-shaped configuration.

Y-X2: Is war a necessary evil?

Y-X1: War is a necessary evil!

Exhibit 44

Y-X1: Y-the digital luminance and colour difference signals in ITV-R601 coding.

Y-X2: Is money really the root of all evil?

Y-X1: Money is the root of all evil!

Exhibit 45

Y-X1: Y- (from CMYK) the third colour of the printing process, (Cyan, Magenta, Yellow and Black) where combined together brings a full colour processing.

Y-X2: Can a human being survive without sex? Is sex a necessity for our bodily functions?

Y-X1: A human being survives without sex! Sex not a necessity for the bodily functions of the human race!

Exhibit 46

Y-X1: Y- or IS, an ancient golf situated in the Southwest region of Zuyderzee in Amsterdam. Today, the region is nearly completely dried. A little part of the Southeast is used as a port.

Y-X2: Is sex and reproduction a necessary evil or can it be avoided?

Y-X1: Sex and reproduction is a necessary evil and can be avoided!

Exhibit 47

Y-X2: Y-lever. The longest lever of a weighbridge to which the steelyard's rod is attached.

Y-X2: Why is it that the only popular -and classical- music that still stand the test of time and sell is music before the year 2000 or even before the nineties?

Y-X1: Only popular -and classical- music still stand the test of time and sell is music before the year 2000 or even before the nineties! It's a question of harmonies and the quantity that has been conceived and it is difficult to create new and different harmonies.

Exhibit 48

Y-X1: Y-2K The Millennium Bug

Y-X2: Y2K2 = 2020 = Y++

Y-X1: Hoaxes, make-beliefs and breaking news. How can we trust anything anyone is saying?